Garden for Magic Creatures

A. Iles

Published by A. Iles, 2024.

GARDEN FOR MAGIC CREATURES

First edition. September 3, 2024.

Copyright © 2024 A. Iles.

ISBN: 979-8227596024

Written by A. Iles.

Table of Contents

For everyone who has seen the wee folk hiding under
the hostas.

Introduction

EVER SINCE RAY DECHOA interviewed me for 106.7 FM's special, 'WIZ' (Witches in Zoogeography), I have been inundated with letters. Listeners have begged me to write a book on my expert knowledge about creating habitat for magical creatures. Residential gardens, as I stated in that interview, are perfect areas for witching folk to welcome magical creatures through habitat design. The witching community needs a guide to help novices and expert gardeners alike! Nearly all of us have access to an outdoor space, in varying sizes, where we can create a unique home for magical creatures great and small.

The amount of information on such a wide-ranging topic would boggle the mind of most witching folk who often know as little about gardening as a celestial fish knows about the deadly sting of an Occisor Musa! This guide will offer helpful advice for beginners, such as planting the deadly Occisor Musa in an area out of reach of children. A seasoned gardener may also learn a thing or two from the information contained in these pages.

For a complete list of all the magical creatures mentioned herein, flip to the back of the guide. A brief description of each species has been included. Every species will demonstrate qualities that are not included here. To give a full description of each, its eating habits, habitat, the geographical spread, and mating culture would be enough to fill several books. This is designed as a primer.

Any witch or warlock can read this guide and take away enough information to make a pretty good space for magical creatures. We are not striving for perfection. If you get most of the way to a diverse garden, then you have done more than the vast majority of witching folk! If striving for perfection prevents you from taking any steps until you are already an expert, then your quest for perfection will leave you with none of the work done.

Magical groves, woodland sanctuaries, enchanted ponds, mystic rivers, and other important areas are bearing a large burden. Smaller and smaller spaces must now play host to all our untamable magical creatures. This is your opportunity to make a counter-cultural change. By creating habitat in your garden, you will make a material difference to the species who take up residence there. We can all participate in improving the habitability of our gardens.

In a wider context, your garden forms part of a network of land that nymphs, faeries, sprites, gnomes, and fire toads can use to travel freely in search of food and shelter. This mobility protects our enchanted brethren by offering them a more diverse breeding pool than if habitats were separated by barriers such as roadways and farmland.

While MagiZoogeography includes a practice of placing important wild spaces under magical protection (to avoid interference from Mundunces*), we are under too much pressure. There are far more Mundunces than there are of us, and they continue to convert wild spaces into enormous fields which are unable to support robust, diverse life.

*Mundunce refers to nonmagical people. It is my understanding that this term is local to my region and that different terms are used around the globe with the same meaning.

It falls upon us, individual members of the witching community, to take part in a revolution. We may not be able to stop the Mundunces, but we can certainly preserve the spaces we have. And if we have no wild spaces to protect? We shall create them!

Many wizarding families have a tradition of passing on their family home to the younger generation. Some of those reading this will have at least a small parcel of family land to call their Garden. Family outcasts, or the youngest of a family of fourteen siblings, may find themselves with little more than a balcony or a windowsill upon which to start. Do not let this discourage you! Small gardens may be limited in their ability to host creatures, but there is no cause for despair!

With patience, in a few years, magical beings will discover your tiny garden. Your Wild Bergamot could become the rest stop for a weary travelling faery. Flavaque Feram, a respected herbologist, studied balcony gardens for five years. The results were most encouraging. The average balcony garden was visited by no less than twenty-five *different species* of magical creatures during the course of the summer months. In addition to these creatures, many more mundane species of insects, birds and mammals also stopped for shade, food, or rest.

A common complaint among Mundunce neighbours of such gardens were the frequent theft of hot chili peppers. Fire toads are particularly fond of spicy vegetables. Happily,

Mundunces are glad to place the blame upon ordinary squirrels and remain none the wiser.

Here we will discuss garden design, habitat creation, the best plants for attracting interesting creatures, how to deal with issues of pests, and tips for garden maintenance. I hope to open your eyes to what Ella Solani would never touch upon in her wildly patronizing six-hundred-page gardening book titled, "Nature Tamed, Grow your Lawn with One Simple Potion." This is for the perfectionist and the hands-off gardener. As long as you have a love for creatures and plants, you are in safe hands.

Also included are tips should you have to deal with the hybrid offspring of two creatures your children have somehow managed to breed illegally beneath the garden shed.

For a garden filled with joy, potion ingredients, life, and food: read on!

-A. ILES, a.k.a., Alfurius Iltorpinder Lethridge Ebruli Starlange

Chapter One

Garden Design

THE FOLLOWING CHAPTER contains a series of tips and
ideas to get you started with garden design. If you would like

to explore the topic more thoroughly, please refer to Tersus Servetur's book 'Garden Planning for Oafs and Halfwits'.

Perhaps it is a sense of responsibility to the MagiEnvironmental community that you are motivated to create habitat. You want to ensure there are enough havens for magical creatures, and you recognize that you can be part of the solution. You have the power to make real change right there in your back garden, on your patio, and on your windowsill!

Large numbers of witching families elect to have the most unremarkable gardens. A smooth velvety green lawn that belongs on a golfing estate is hardly conducive to the joys that seeing unicorns and fauns can offer! Perfectly trimmed evergreen topiaries are little better. Sure, minotaurs love them; they are striking and aesthetically pleasing enough. But aside from a small space where birds can perch, these topiaries are useful only as a display of wealth.

I like to think that if I were rich enough to own a large estate, I would not keep it so trimmed and *proper* simply to show off to my neighbours! Goodness knows, walking in a meadow of wildflowers, or through a densely wooded area, or even around a well-tended garden does the soul a lot of good! Why bother having such a large property if you cannot leave your front door without seeing the traffic on the street below, or having your neighbours staring at you from their own expanse of uninterrupted lawn? Planting trees for privacy is a bare minimum for a comfortable home!

Please, hold onto your panic. I will not ask you to convert your entire garden into a wild, untamed mass of plants gone to seed! Habitat for magical creatures does not have to look careless. If it is not your wish to let plants revert to nature, then it shall not be so! We can create an area devoted to magical creatures that is separate from your fancy topiaries and your boring lawn.

The easiest way to maintain a semblance of order is to plant in rows or repeating patterns. Such gardens enjoy looking mundane enough to pass unnoticed by Mundunce neighbours. This can please the witching family who believes such things as Other People's Opinions are worthy of note. Rows do not have to be perfectly straight, but they are easier to maintain when they are. You could have curving rows in your borders, or plant different species and varieties within the same row. See below for an example of how straight rows can both create habitat *and* look orderly:

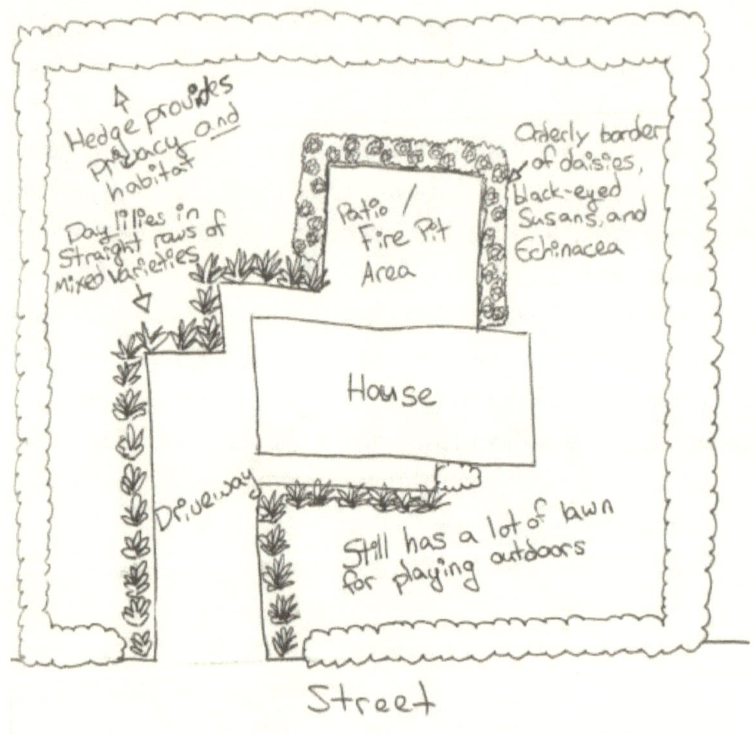

IN THE IMAGE ABOVE, habitat is provided in several ways. Hedges offer protection from inclement weather. Borders of mixed flowers provide food, nectar, and nesting opportunities. Leprechauns, gnomes, and brownies will burrow between daylilies which provide the perfect cover.

Another favourite strategy of mine is to plant in clumps. If I have a tree in the middle of a garden, I want to take advantage of every inch of space I have to increase the diversity of plants I can provide to creatures. Since I do not have a large garden, the space around the trunk of a tree (where there is too much shade for most flowers) is an interesting challenge. Or an opportunity!

Since spring bulbs grow and hibernate so early, a ring of crocuses around a tree can be a fantastic addition to the garden. By the time the tree's leaves begin to shade the ground, the crocuses have finished their short life cycle and returned their precious sugars to their underground bulb. Their early blooms cheer on the spring, and their eye-catching colours will draw faeries from far and wide.

Or, if you want large, lush leaves all summer long, a ring of shade-loving hostas around the base of a tree could attract a gnome family. The huge leaves make excellent shelters from rain, and pixies love the perfumed white and purple flowers that bloom in late summer. Hostas are also edible for us—the young shoots that appear in early spring are a delicious vegetable!

You can plant in rings around the base of trees, or in clumps in the middle of an otherwise dull lawn. Faeries are particularly fond of rings. If you wish to make an offering to faeries, there is no better place than in a sacred circle. Here is an example of how integrating plants into a space currently occupied by a lawn could look:

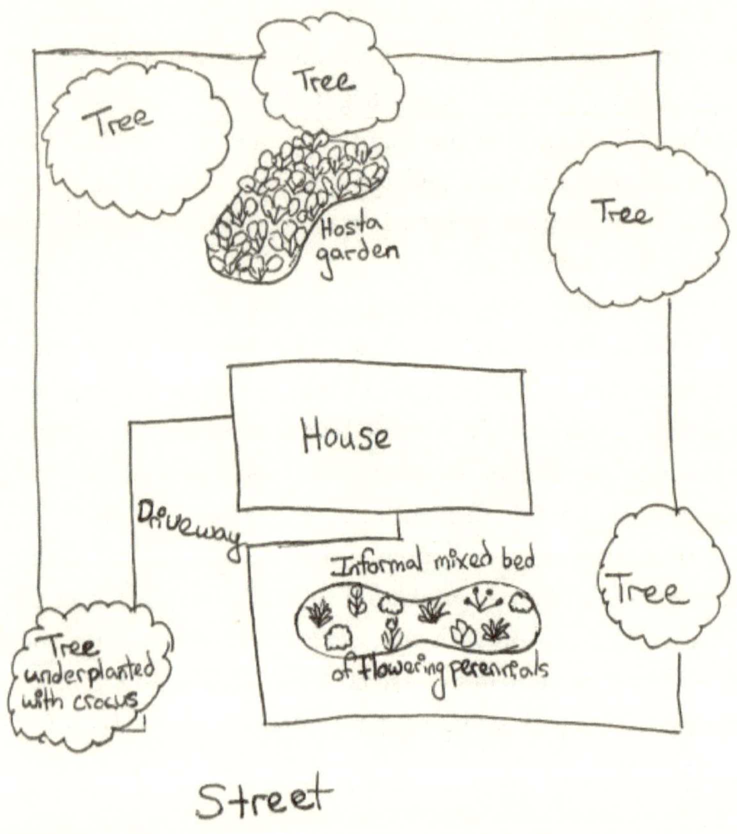

IN THE EXAMPLE ABOVE, you can see habitat created in the tree canopies, under the trees, in the mixed beds of flowering perennials, and in the hosta garden. Indeed, the only place unsuitable for creature habitat besides the street, house, and driveway is the lawn. The lawn is the enemy of diversity.

When planting trees into your landscape, there are many options. You could plant trees that will live hundreds of years and grow big enough to cast shade on your home. Or, trees that bear nuts. You could plant fruiting bushes which will provide food for your family as well as food and habitat for creatures and animals. You could even plant trees for strictly ornamental purposes! Some will flower impressively in the spring and summer. Give it some thought, once a tree is planted you will not want to move it.

Bear in mind with the above strategy, you are intending to maintain a lawn between the habitat gardens. As such, if you have several circles of plants, you need to ensure that you are leaving enough space between them to pass with a lawnmower. Not just at planting time; plants grow and multiply. Over time, the little clump you planted may betwice the size you initially intended. Leave enough room to maintain the lawn between them.

By planting in patterns or rows, you keep the semblance of order. The animals and creatures we want to attract are usually smaller than we are. Their view of the garden is vastly different than ours. To a pixie, a shrub is a skyscraper filled with adventure, possibility, and danger.

If they find nectar, insects, mushrooms, and comfortable places to sleep, creatures will be more than happy to adapt to whichever garden design you have elected. If you can introduce a small pond to your garden, you will be blessed with even more creatures. Brownies are particularly fond of fishing for tadpoles, while water sprites and ashrays only live in water.

I invite you to look at your garden practically. Many novices are either so excited or dimwitted that they merely toss seeds into the air and expect the garden to sort itself out. I have visited elderly witching folk who see nothing wrong with having radishes growing right next to a dangerous plant.

Imagine the peril of being bent over, harvesting a radish, and a Scalpere Vine is mischievously waiting for you to step into its reach. This plant has stems capable of moving very quickly in its quest to find tender flesh to cut into and consume. Or, a child may be picking basil leaves for the evening salad, and accidentally pick leaves from aconite. The whole family could die because of a simple oversight with the garden design!

It falls onto me to implore you to separate your edible plants from your hazardous plants. There are many ornamental plants that are edible. Focus on giving poisonous or violent plants their own space in the garden. This way, children and guests can be made aware that some areas are not designed to be explored by unwary victims.

Once you've successfully transplanted your dangerous and semi-conscious plants to their own area of the garden, I suggest breaking up the other species into sections based on use. Potion-making plants could be grouped together (either in rows, or clumps). It is convenient when making a Sleeping Potion to know where to find your Catswort and other necessary ingredients—all in one place.

Tea-making plants can have their own border. Vegetables for human consumption should be kept well apart from the garden dedicated to habitat (unless you want gnomes eating them all!).

Creating several smaller gardens also adds to the illusion of control that Mundunces are so fond of. Even I must admit there is something tranquil about looking at tidy rows in a weed-free garden. Here are two examples of how you could create separate gardens within your lot:

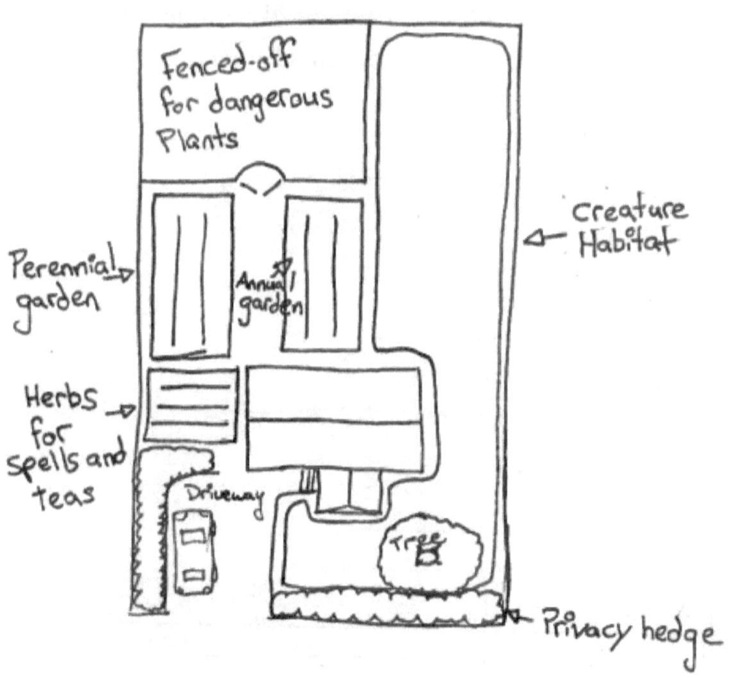

Fenced-off for dangerous Plants
Perennial garden
Annual garden
Herbs for spells and teas
creature Habitat
Driveway
Tree
Privacy hedge

The section labeled creature habitat will be explored in further detail in subsequent chapters.

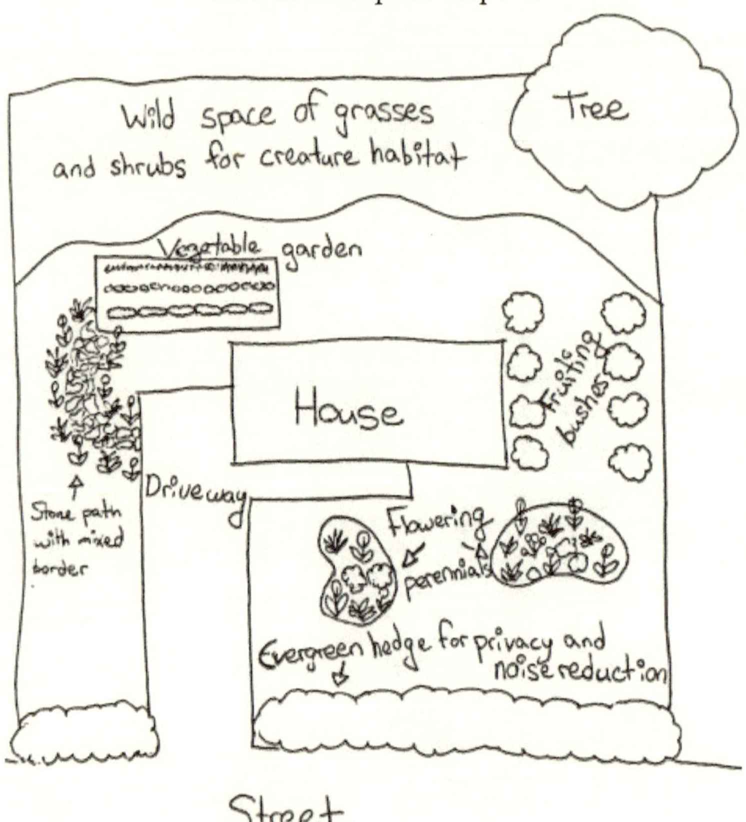

EDIBLE PLANTS CAN BE either annual (plants that must be replanted at least yearly) or perennial (plants that return on their own, year after year). My preference is to plant annuals in their own garden bed. This makes soil preparation simple. You can clean off all plant debris from the garden at the same time in the fall. Then, you may till the whole area in the spring. When greedy gnomes and flea beetles threaten to eat your growing vegetables, they are easy to protect with a floating row-cover if they are all planted in a straight bed.

Since the perennials remain year after year, tilling around their sensitive roots would damage the plants. Having annuals growing alongside perennials puts the annuals at a disadvantage; the perennial plants' roots are larger and can take up water and nutrients faster than unestablished annuals. It is best to keep them separated.

In this system, your bobble cherries and rhubarb will be kept to one area of the garden while your potatoes, onions, and carrots belong in another. I will not get into the details of pruning plants in this book as Haud Pupator did an excellent job detailing everything you need to know in his exhaustive book, 'Encyclopedia of Pruning All That Grows from Mundane to Magical and Anything in Between Including Aquatic Plants of the Antarctic and Highland Brush of the Equator and Also Frigid Plants of the Global North' (someone should have told him to edit that title).

Now that you have all the essential elements in your garden, you can carve out an area for that most unselfish goal—biodiversity and resilience. This section of your garden will be the focus of the rest of this guide. This is where you will incorporate all the plants that attract beings magical and mundane. You may also find projects here to distract your children, such as building houses and hotels for these precious creatures (thus earning yourself a few hours of peace from the incessant nattering of your offspring).

The area of your garden dedicated to preserving our natural allies can be as varied as the plants and habitats you choose to place within it. Your garden can be anything! It could be on the edge of a forest, riverside, or pond. It could contain a hedgerow, wildflower meadow, or scorched piece of earth after a hot fire. You might design a traditional cottage garden or maximize space on a patio and create a vertical garden. You could be planting in a desert, on a rooftop, or even a greenhouse of exotic plants that would be unable to grow in your climate without skillful care.

The plants you choose and the habitats you create will influence which creatures are most likely to appear there. Every plant and every patch of earth is a potential home for beings magical and mundane, and the insects that feed them.

It is time to get to work. Make a list of all the elements already in your garden, and the normal climate conditions. Many gardeners spend hours every week carefully tending a huge diversity of plants.

I have a secret for you: you do not need to grow every species of plant ever discovered on the face of the earth to be a good gardener! That list of existing elements you just wrote—those are your strengths!

Find plants that *thrive* in those specific conditions. It will save you much of the hassle of frequent watering, protecting tender plants from early frosts, and seasonal infestations. Choose plants that are robustly well adapted to your area. You live in a desert? Great! Look for succulents and cacti. You live in a humid environment? Try orchids and ferns!

If you find that your near-arctic conditions limit you to only a handful of super-hardy sedums adapted to growing in USDA Zone 2, so be it. My advice is that you do not fight nature, enhance it! Magical creatures live in every environment. They are as diverse as animals, each culture is familiar with its own creatures and myths. You can occasionally manipulate the conditions of nature a little, but your time as a gardener can be more enjoyable if your plants are not constantly facing the threats of disease and climate pressures.

Even if you only plant ten species of plants, you can still enjoy the visits of many creatures.

If you can only plant five species, I guarantee you the same thing! Remember, many of our favourite garden ornamentals have been bred extensively over the years. If you can only grow monarda and hemerocallis, do not despair. These hardy perennials come in so many different colours, sizes, and blooming times that you can create a special oasis just using those two species.

A final thought on garden design: you may consider planting a thick hedge of shrubs or bushes around the perimeter of your property. These will bring privacy to your garden and allow you to do whatever you want without drawing the attention of conformist Mundunces. Also, it is much more pleasant to celebrate Nude Gardening Day when the creepy neighbour across the street cannot see your flabby bits.

Being a good witch or warlock is not about complicating one's life. It is about embracing natural energies and allowing them to flow. So it shall be in the Garden for Magical Creatures!

Chapter Two

Habitats for Magical Creatures

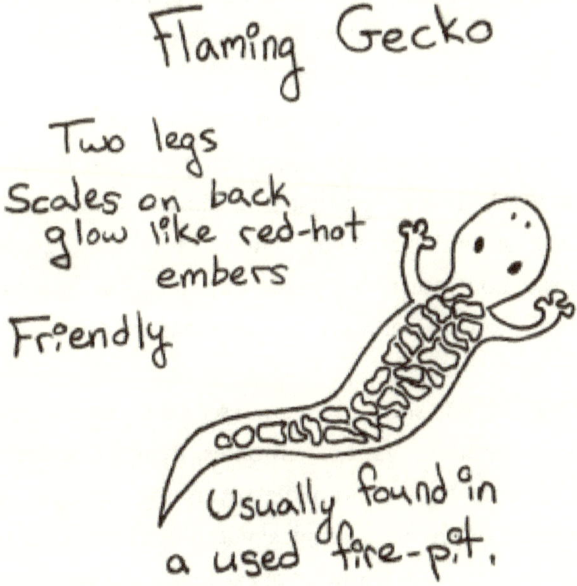

LET'S FACE IT; YOU need help. You want to make the most of your garden's potential life-hosting abilities, but you need to learn some simple facts. Sometimes, less is more. You do not want to overwork a garden meant to provide peace and tranquility. Once the basics are in play, leave it alone!

The last thing you want to do is accidentally overturn a nest of leprechaun young. Such a mishap could result in a curse being placed upon your family tree that hinders you and your descendants from accumulating wealth for the next century. Thank goodness you came to me first, before getting stuck in!

My own garden is a humble one-tenth of an acre. Even so, within ten paces of my back door I have found evidence that a herd of unicorns come to visit. They bite off the tops of my tulips! Their manure is an excellent fertilizer; not quite as visually pleasing as the tulips (even with its rainbow highlights), but it is an acceptable exchange.

A garden the size of my own could never be depended on to supply a herd of unicorns (or even a singular unicorn) with all their needs. It is a sign that your garden has become part of a network of wild spaces large enough to allow these beautiful creatures to continue to live peacefully among us. None of us can be the solution on our own, but together we can contribute to unimaginable change.

In general, you should expect to see smaller creatures making camp in your home garden. Gnomes, nymphs, sprites, faeries, brownies, leprechauns, and pixies are among those you will most likely encounter living in a typical witching family's garden. They are seldom spotted in Mundunce gardens.

Frequent visitors to the garden may include fire birds, phoenixes, cat-sith, chupacabras, harpies, and fauns. While foxes are not always considered magical creatures, I have a soft spot for these and celebrate anytime I am lucky enough to spot one.

Your geographic location is a strong influence when it comes to which creatures you can expect to see. The second strongest influence is the type of food you have on offer. Here, we have some control. For example, golden apples are a staple in the Fire Bird's diet. During autumn months, golden apples are their primary food source. While you may be visited by the Fire Bird even without golden apples, your likelihood of seeing one is much increased if you can supply it with its favourite meal. In such a case, the Fire Bird may remain in your garden for several weeks before continuing its migration.

If you have a few acres of land, you may be able to entice a dragon to stop and rest. They live in mountain ranges, but occasionally venture out to find a mate. Dragons require an open meadow or field in which to land. They will mark these areas as safe landing spaces by burning their family crest upon the ground before they leave. This enables them to find the clearing more easily upon their return journey (Mundunces adorably think these are messages from alien races).

Anyone wanting to play host to dragons and the myriad of other magical creatures specially adapted to grasslands ought to focus on maintaining the habitat. Grasslands are often forgotten when discussing wild spaces. People prefer to speak of forests and wetlands. Every habitat has its value! As mentioned in the previous chapter, your strength will lie in knowing what your particular patch of earth is specifically adapted to.

Flaming Geckos enjoy making a home in patches of burnt earth, as do some birds. A home gardener may replicate this habitat in their own gardens by creating a small, controlled fire and extinguishing it after several hours. Weeks later, you may find a family of Flaming Geckos scurrying out from the ashes.

Unicorns, minotaurs, ogres, sphinxes, and other large magical creatures will visit your garden if you are near a forest, swamp, lake, or meadow.

Similarly, bigfoot and yetis only ever reside in the most remote mountains of the Rockies and Himalayas. Ever since efforts were made to save these creatures from extinction by beginning a crossbreeding program, the yeti of the Himalayas have disappeared altogether. Meanwhile, the bigfoot of the Rockies have achieved a level of intelligence equaling that of witching folk. Thus, it is no longer appropriate to speak of bigfoot in the same sentence as a faun (half goat, half man).

Bigfoot of today are more like witching folk in magical ability and intelligence than any other creature. It was in the news recently that a bigfoot/yeti offspring from the Rockies has been accepted to Kentree Institute of Magic—quite an achievement and the first of its kind!

When gardening for creatures, one must consider two crucial elements: diet and habitat. Here we begin with habitat.

Small magical creatures live either in trees, underground burrows, beneath rocks, the hollow stems of flowers, or in rotting logs. When creating a creature-friendly garden (whether they are magical or mundane!), one should primarily plant perennials. Perennials are planted once, then they are expected to live between ten and five-hundred years.

Since many creatures and the insects and earthworms that make up part of their diet reside beneath the ground, it is important not to disturb the soil with yearly ploughing. By planting perennials, we will not have to disturb the top layer of soil continuously, or remove the all-important layer of decomposing plants on the surface.

For example, the firefly will lay its eggs on decaying organic matter or directly on moist soil. Sometimes the eggs are bioluminescent; you might be lucky enough to spot them. These must remain undisturbed for four weeks until they hatch. The larva looks similar to a worm, and spends its summer hunting slugs and other insects. It will burrow underground in the winter.

Some firefly larva carry on this way for another summer and burrow underground for a second winter before finally entering the pupal stage and emerging as an adult firefly. The firefly's three year cycle is the best example of the importance of leaving areas undisturbed. If we tilled the soil every year and removed all the organic matter, the fireflies would have nowhere to go. They would be crushed by our activities.

When we till the earth, we also run the risk of destroying gnome and leprechaun dwellings. The consequences of destroying the home of a family of leprechauns is worth avoiding. If you like having financial wealth, or aspire to have it someday, it will be nearly impossible after destroying a leprechaun burrow.

The decaying leaves on the surface of the soil have the important job of supporting fungi, which are a vital source of nutrition for gnomes, faeries, and pixies alike. If you wish to see a brownie hopping around between anthills, you need to have a healthy network of mushrooms. These mushrooms have intricate underground networks that aid plants in accessing precious nutrients. Thus, there are many reasons not to disturb the balance in the soil.

Keep in mind the particular needs of the creatures you wish to host. All creatures need shelter. For those who prefer to hide among rocks (like lizards), keep a small pile of stones in a corner of your garden. Maximize the use of your space. The rock pile is best suited where the soil is of such poor quality, or so compacted, that it cannot support plant life. Creatures can hide among the rocks on a rainy day, or cool off in the shade when it is sunny. Luminescent Snakes may moon bathe upon the stones on a cloudless night.

There is another question to consider. Do you want your garden to be a welcoming space for Mundunces? Or do you want to make it a space that will inspire terror? I dream of someday designing a garden using only black and dark purple blooms and foliage. A perpetually ominous space filled with the most dangerous and poisonous plants I can get my hands on. My grandchildren visit too often for me to realize this dream at home, but perhaps someday...

We have all heard the saying "as exciting as watching grass grow." In the case of some magical and mundane beings—this is actually very exciting indeed! Unicorns and rabbits love to graze upon the tender shoots of grass and clover. Tall grass is a great hideaway for smaller creatures that fall prey to eagles and owls. Imagine being three inches tall—the grass makes an instant jungle gym where young pixies can play!

Leaving the grass to grow beyond a few inches may look like a travesty to your neighbours. They probably wish you would stop trying to look so peculiar. Flowers begin to sprout among the mess, and Mundunces have a peculiar hatred for that beautiful yellow flower; the dandelion. Yet it is a favourite for faeries who use the white fluffy pappus to hitch a ride to different gardens!

I have a strategy for discouraging your neighbours' disparaging comments; let them know you are protecting the planet. Nothing shuts people up as much as an outward display of moral superiority!

A small pile of logs, preferably topped up yearly to maintain a constant range of decomposition, is a perfect habitat for creatures and fungi. Some tree nymphs prefer to hide among the logs rather than sleep in the canopy of a tree, and they require them for winter hibernation. The logs also provide food for insects, which in turn provide food for the creatures you are harbouring.

The circle of life does not discriminate between magical and mundane. More often than not, I have found that the two depend on one another more than some would believe. Sometimes, when I encourage witching folk to incorporate more Mundunce practices into their gardens they get offended. They send trolls to my home to 'teach me a lesson.'

I am always prepared to offer trolls a meal of Termite Cakes, which never fails to placate them. My critics are better off not wasting their time. It cannot be helped that the same insects that feed goblins also feed hedgehogs. I will hardly pretend that I think a goblin is better company that the adorable hedgehog.

Trees and shrubs are essential elements in habitats for wood nymphs and sprites. The type of trees you plant will influence who decides to move in. Wood nymphs are as varied as any other creature. Some prefer hardwood, others search for evergreens, and a few choose fruit trees exclusively. You will find some prefer a low shrub, and others inhabit places where trees reach over fifty feet tall.

Leprechauns love boots. While they will happily create subterranean burrows, they can also be tempted to make a home using old boots or shoes. They are fond of anything that sparkles.

If you place a mound of glittering stones next to an old shoe, a leprechaun couple will surely be sitting outside smoking a pipe of tobacco in a matter of weeks. Give it a few months, and they will be planting a small batch of miniature barley and wheat.

With a pond or a stream, all forms of beasties will bathe there. Never forget that creatures are a little meat-headed. They can dive headfirst into a pond without a thought to how they will get back out of the water. A wooden plank, sloping sides, a rocky ramp, or a rope ladder that can aid stranded creatures come out of the water will be instrumental to their safety and happiness. It is traumatizing to a six-year-old to discover their pixie friends face down on the surface of a shallow pond they could not escape. Traumatic enough that in my case it propelled me into a career of creating appropriate creature habitats.

Ponds offer another service, apart from bathing; You may find it becoming home to aquatic species! These can include the ashray, grindylow, kappa, and kelpie. They will be very grateful if you provide them with a semi-submerged stone or raft upon which they can sunbathe without venturing out onto land where they are easy prey.

Your gnomes might take up fishing as a hobby. A pond stocked with minnows or tadpoles provides opportunity for this sport. Gnomes are partial to cooking their catch on a small fire. They are responsible fishermen, and I've never known them to over-fish a pond. Water sprites will eat gnomes careless enough to fall prey to their tricks. A note of caution; never follow the water sprites' lights.

Keep in mind that the pond is not the only source of drinking water. Many creatures, insects, and animals will prefer drinking morning dew from leaves of plants or nectar from a flower before sucking water from a muddy pond. Even so, to prevent the pond from becoming a stagnant breeding ground for mosquitoes, I recommend a Fountain Charm to keep water circulating and oxygenated.

Chapter Three

Plants and Foods for Magical Creatures

NOW WE FIND OURSELVES looking at which plants are most adept at attracting our enchanted brethren. Rather than listing creatures or plants alphabetically, which is hard to assimilate, or creating a chart where you can cross-reference creatures to plants, I have decided to outline some fool-proof rules of thumb. Included is a brief list of suggested plantings for you, based on their wide range of adaptation. Your geographic region is unknown to me, so I have tried to select plants that thrive in diverse conditions. The harshness of your winter, the amount of rainfall, the heat of your summer, and the quality of your soil will ultimately determine the most suitable plants for your garden. This chapter will help you get started.

If you go to a local garden center and ask for help, you can certainly find a good dozen plants with which to start experimenting. You do not have to create the entire garden in your first year. Choose a section of your land where you want to start and do what you can. Each year you can add to it, if you chose. Gain confidence, set a budget, and pat yourself on the back for doing something great for the planet. When you learn to propagate plants, you can begin to exchange them with your neighbours and continue to fill your garden without over-extending your finances.

Not interested in any gardening at all? A simple way to increase biodiversity and habitat without spending time, money, or energy is simply to leave a section of your lawn un-mowed. This is easy and 100% effective, but it does not help fill the pages of a book! By allowing your lawn to grow, wildflowers and trees will seed themselves and grow unchecked. It might look messy, but it works!

Many of the plants that belong in a magical garden are the same plants that can be found in any Mundunce garden center. Magic qualities and usefulness in potions are widespread in the plant kingdom. I have frequently been shocked at how readily available Monkshood is for Mundunces, even though this plant is surely fatal to them. The odds are good that you will encounter a beginner witch in a garden center. An affinity with plants is often the first sign that someone is beginning to manifest their powers on a higher level.

A good starting point when shopping for plants would be to purchase a few varieties of flowers. Pixies and nymphs enjoy drinking nectar and pixies like to hide in tall grasses among the stems of wildflowers. For best results choose purple, pink, or red flowers. They are eye-catching enough to be seen from a long distance. Pixies flying overhead will spot them and come to rest. Be warned, pixies hate blue or green flowers. They will tear and destroy them to make more room for their favourite flowers to grow.

In the case of faeries and fire birds, both enjoy a selection of fruit. Fire birds will feast on golden apples but will eat other fruit when apples are not available. Cherries, crab apples, and berries of any kind will encourage these to visit and perhaps even make a home in your garden. Faeries enjoy yellow flowers and they use pollen to dye their locks a golden yellow. It has also been noted that faeries adore plantings of blue flowers and protect them fiercely. It has been theorized that they only do this because they know it enrages the pixies.

Sprites rely on nectar far more than pixies (who also enjoy munching on leaves, insects, and fruits). Sprites love red flowers most of all, though they will settle for other brightly coloured flowers if there are no red ones available. Bell or cone shaped flowers are especially appealing to the sprites who have long tongues capable of reaching nectar that other creatures cannot.

The plants I suggest here are widespread (meaning they can grow in many climate zones) and easy to maintain. They have a high potential of attracting nymphs, brownies, pixies, faeries, and sprites.

- Monarda; also known as bee balm or wild bergamot. This plant has a delicate fragrance and eruptive red flowers filled with sweet nectar. It makes a good tea, attracts sprites and hummingbirds, and will quickly spread by seed or underground. There are many varieties available which come in different colours.

- Columbine; a great flower to kick off the spring. Comes in many colours and grows in partially shady gardens. Versatile and great for attracting faeries.

- Echinacea; also known as cone flower, their long-lasting blooms come in many colours and are rich in nectar. They attract bees, butterflies, and sprites. The roots can be harvested as a potions ingredient.

- Foxglove; elegant spikes of purple and pink flowers. These are not technically perennials but they will self-seed. This ensures the continuous return of these delightful plants.

- Hemerocallis; the leaves are nothing to write home about. It looks like tall, overgrown grass. The magic happens in mid-summer when large trumpet-shaped flowers emerge in quantity. Each flower lasts only a day, hence their common name 'daylily', but they produce dozens of flowers per plant. Their bloom time lasts a few weeks, and you can get these tough, widely adapted plants in every colour.

- Hollyhock; large round flowers are very attractive

though the plant is often an eye-sore while not in bloom. They come in varying colours, I have one whose flowers are black as night.

- Sedums; also known as stonecrop, these fleshy succulents are usually edible. The flowers are excellent at attracting all manner of magical and mundane creatures, and the plants can grow large and bushy, or as small ground cover. While the foliage is not my favourite to look at, some sedums flower in the fall when many other flowers have faded, which makes them a welcome addition to any garden.

- Lavender; use this fragrant plant to attract creatures, make teas, or use in potions. Compact plant will not spread quickly.

- Lupine; a truly spectacular display of flowers and the star-shaped leaves are always delightful.

- Clover; an alternative to grass. If you have a lawn, be sure to sprinkle some low-growing clover seeds into your yard. The small flowers provide nectar and the plant itself is nutritious for rabbits, deer, and unicorns.

- Catswort; also known as catnip. Great for sleeping draughts, attracting felines, and repelling mosquitoes. Just rub the fresh leaf on your skin and get a few hours of relief from those hideous insects. The tiny purple flowers are a favourite for bees and nymphs.

- Lemon balm; looks somewhat like mint but produces a most refreshing lemon-y aroma. Tiny flowers attract many creatures and pollinators.

- Allium; Hardy, perennial, drought-tolerant, and very attractive to creatures magical and mundane. They come in so many varieties, you could have alliums big and small flowering from April to November.

Brownies, gnomes, and leprechauns stay close to the ground and eat fleshy creatures that dwell there. Brownies are especially fond of small fish which they catch from the edge of a pond using small fishing rods made of twigs and hair. Gnomes bully brownies and steal their fishing rods. If there are no brownies available to steal from, gnomes will eat worms, bugs, and mushrooms. Brownies have a tendency to be scavengers and will most likely be found in your compost heap, having a boxing match over your potato peels and other kitchen scraps.

Ogres will find their way into muddy puddles, so be careful not to cultivate your vegetable garden before a heavy rain. You may have to start the work all over again after an ogre has rolled around. If the spring remains wet, the ogre will be unwilling to leave until the muddy patch of earth has completely dried out. Timing is crucial when it comes to tilling.

Ogres dislike anything colourful. Some people have suggested planting flowers near the vegetable patch, but I find ogres are intelligent enough to pull these out. Painting the garden shed a bright colour is another theory I am afraid I must refute. Ogres are not nearly as dimwitted as we expect them to be. They will soon have that brightly coloured garden shed painted with a thick layer of mud if you are lucky, or completely dismantled and eaten if you are unlucky.

Flaming geckos and other reptiles are not so common in my area; I cannot state firsthand how they behave in a garden. I can advise you that having drought-tolerant plants (succulents, cacti, and grasses), climbing vines, and sunning stones will be much appreciated by these creatures. If you want to get more amusement from your garden, have a small square of sand in a sunny spot. When a lizard walks across it, they will leave footprints and tail patterns. Even if you don't see the lizards with your own eyes, you will know they were there! Since many of these creatures depend on insects for their diets, it is essential to provide those insects with habitat (rotting logs, bug hotels).

Chimaera, cat-sith, and sphinxes come from distinctly different parts of the world so it may offend a few readers to see them grouped into one category. The harsh truth is that these magnificent animals all share feline ancestry which makes it very likely you will come across these fellows rolling around in your Catswort. Planting Catswort will also attract the housecats of the neighbourhood.

The only issue with having feline visitors in your garden is that their diet includes birds, mammals, creatures, fish, and small children. Manticore have the incredible ability to bite into any plant—no matter how covered it is in spines! Cacti are a favourite part of their diet, but they will even venture to eat such plants as the aforementioned Scalpere Vine!

If watching a unicorn from your balcony is your ultimate dream, then you will be waiting for them with grasses, clover, alfalfa, or shrubs upon which they can browse. They particularly like eating unopened flower buds, the tips of growing branches, and hostas. They dazzle in the sunshine, but often stick to the shade in order to avoid being seen. A unicorn spotted by moonlight is one of the greatest joys any nature-lover can hope to experience.

A sure way to attract unicorns if you do not have an apple tree is to throw a few apples into the garden once a week. Vanity is rampant among unicorns. A garden feature sporting mirrors is sure to command their attention, even when apples are nowhere to be found.

Dragon habitat has already been discussed, but what do dragons eat? If you want to see one of these scaly monsters descend into your meadow there is one way to attract them: livestock. Dragons have a fondness for sheep, a fondness which I share. The downside is that a single dragon can eat as many as twelve sheep in one day. It's not feasible to dream of having one as a pet.

One final note for this chapter. It is my understanding that children who have yet to learn to control their magic tend to use it for perverted designs. Whether this is because children are naturally bent toward causing chaos, or whether it is purely accidental every time I dare not say (though I have my suspicions). Nevertheless, it is a common occurrence that around young children, new species of magical creatures are accidentally bred. How this cross-breeding happens is a mystery, but a child always appears at the root of it.

Before you allow any of these strange mutations to grow to maturity, I implore you to contact your local magical authority about their removal. You may tell your child the creatures they created have gone to stay on a farm. What your child does not need to know is that the farm is a dragon farm, and those horrible little hybrids are destined to be the food.

Chapter Four

Edible Garden

Gnomes

IT IS POSSIBLE TO HAVE a garden for creatures as well as a garden for sustenance. However, one should be aware that creatures are naughty wee things and can behave mischievously when they want to. The best way to avoid difficulty is to plan for disaster. The alternative is to wait for disaster and then spend the rest of the year crying out "woe is me," while trying to eradicate these special pests from your property.

Let's start in the spring, when the year in the garden begins. Vegetable gardens need to be dug over. This is an excellent time to remove weeds which would compete with your crops and incorporate fertilizer into the earth. Tilling provides the perfect airy conditions for seeds to sprout.

The soil will be ready for planting when it is crumbly in texture and neither soggy nor bone dry. Fertilizer is essential for growing most vegetables, but some are heavier feeders than others. Sweet peas need relatively little additional fertility when compared to a heavy feeder like cabbage or corn.

Manure is a potent fertilizer and should only be used in measured quantities. Bat, dragon, ogre, and manticore manure are those which have the highest levels of Nitrogen. This is excellent for leafy growth. The next best manure comes from pheasants, ostriches, fire birds, fish, and gnomes. Manure must always be spread with care. Quantity matters.

Why?

Too many nutrients can burn delicate young roots. The nutrients that are not absorbed into the soil (if you have applied too much or right before a heavy rain) can leach off into waterways. This results in killing all plants and animals in the waterways through a process that begins with algae bloom and ends when there is no useable oxygen in the water.

This process is so widely understood that even Mundunces, who pretend not to see anything unless it is directly beneath their noses, have noticed and documented it. This book will not dive in depth into the application of all fertilizers, but I do have one key rule that will help you. You will not learn all there is to know about manure application, but a quick rule of thumb will keep you on the right track.

Novice gardeners are far better off buying a *composted* manure, or compost mix.

Before you decide to dump raw animal feces onto the patch of earth where you are growing your food, you should understand that there are potential consequences. With a well-rotted, composted manure this risk is eliminated. Compost contains nutrients in a more stable form than raw manure. In a compost, the manure and other feedstocks have already been decomposed to the point of stability.

This means the nutrients in the compost are less likely to pose a leaching risk since there are more stable organic matter surfaces for the nutrients to adhere to. Here, they can stay available for the plants while remaining less volatile and mobile. When applying raw manure, you even lose nutrients to the atmosphere—that's how unstable it is!

Raw manure should never be applied where you intend to harvest a vegetable that has come into contact with the soil less than one-hundred eighty days after manure application. Though you may argue lettuce is not technically in contact with the soil, splashes caused by rain can move raw manure onto the leaves and cause E-Coli sickness for humans and creatures. There are potions to ease these ailments, but it is best to avoid the illness altogether. As many witching families have close relationships with their Mundunce neighbours, I feel it is my duty to warn you that Mundunce bodies are far more fragile than magical ones and can become very ill if a ham-handed mage is not careful. Better use my rule of thumb:

Use compost, then forget about it.

The next important step in the edible garden is to protect your crops from teeth that do not belong to your family.

Leprechauns are especially drawn to potatoes. The best way to ensure absolute protection is to build a wooden frame and cover the vegetable patch with galvanized chicken wire. Leprechauns find the zinc in galvanized wire repulsive. If you intend on having only a very small garden you could do this fairly easily.

In my case, instead of covering the garden and waging territory wars with creatures, I grow enough that I will not be disappointed when a portion is eaten by animals and creatures. By doing this, my garden is always over-productive for my own needs. I over-estimate when I plant how much I can physically eat in a year, then I can share the bounty. This is a matter of preference. I have never gone hungry and we all live together harmoniously this way.

There are some exceptions to this rule. I can be a little over-protective of my strawberries and arugula. A simple floating row-cover provides enough of a barrier for most pesky creatures. In this way, I never have to resort to cruel potions to remove beasties from my cabbages and I never have to worry that I could later ingest a portion of the potion which remains on my food.

It is common knowledge that magical and semi-magical beings are more delicious than mundane ones. Pork, coming from the most mundane of animals, is barely edible when you compare it to the effervescent flesh of a phoenix. I have heard that great men weep from the delightful flavour of a faun. Unicorns and dragons are applauded for meat of such complexity and balance that we can scarcely comprehend the delight being experienced in our mouths. Most witching folk rightly swear off the consumption of any of these rare animals.

Happily, there are plenty of semi-magical beings who are delicious without making one question the morality of eating them. Pheasant, guinea fowl, and peacocks are among the most common livestock in witching families' gardens. These birds are intelligent enough to avoid razor sharp vines and huge carnivorous plants. They enjoy chowing down on gnomes; this prevents the population from getting too high.

Chickens and turkeys are supremely stupid and best kept to a coop with a dedicated range. They are vulnerable to dangers in a garden filled with potential predators.

There is a trend rising in popularity among witching folk to avoid eating meat altogether. For reasons of environmental protection they have surmised that animal agriculture and the growing of crops to support it has a heavy role to play in the issues our planet is undergoing (extreme weather, etc.). The theory is that without animal agriculture less land would need to be converted to growing crops. This would fare well for magical creatures, too.

There are many delicious plants that can replace the need for animal flesh, and anyone who truly cares about creating a habitat for animals should consider joining this revolution. My own household continues to enjoy the pleasures of meat, but we have cut down to twice a week. Again, doing *something* is better than doing nothing at all. Were it not for my spouse's moaning, I would be able to remove meat from my diet for all but the most special occasions. If you currently eat meat three meals a day, I might suggest reducing it to just one meal. If you eat meat once a day, consider reducing to once every other day. Do what you can and the whole world will benefit.

If you are a tea-drinker, like me, you will want to have a section of your garden dedicated to fragrant herbs. Among my favourites for taste are lemon balm, wild bergamot, and sage.

If you have trouble sleeping, I recommend catswort, but the flavour is unpleasant so I always combine it with mint to cover the bitterness.

When a woman suffers menstrual cramps, she can make use of raspberry leaves to brew a flavourful tea which reduces the inflammation and pain. I always harvest and dry enough raspberry leaves to get me through the winter.

All the above-named teas will leave you with a yellow/green drink. I amuse myself by adding a few flowers to get a nice colour. Hibiscus, red clover or wild bergamot flowers can lend a pleasant red or purple hue if used in large enough quantities. The flowers also carry small amounts of nectar that can act as natural sweetener. Lavender makes a wonderful olfactory addition to tea, but does little to change the flavour.

When it comes to potion making, there are many herbs and plants you could bring into your garden to aid in this art. Personally, I have never taken much of a liking to potion-making as it requires perfectionism beyond my natural inclination. You will be in safe hands if you reference Paul Dominum's book 'Cultivation, Harvest, and Storage of Most Common Potions Ingredients.' It is a comprehensive guide of annual and perennial herbs, their function, and the correct time to harvest.

I have never understood why sage harvested at midnight under a crescent moon would have the power to banish a poltergeist while sage harvested at any other time only has the power to cure sore throats and flavour soup. Then again, the whole of what I do not know is enough to fill several libraries. Rest assured you will be better served consulting an expert on potions in this case. I am nothing more than a specialist gardener

who knows too much about the behaviour and genitals of
magical creatures great and small.

46

Chapter Five

Maintenance and Propagation

ONCE YOU REACH A CRITICAL mass of creatures, many
species are able to maintain a garden by themselves (to their own

liking). They will replant the seeds of their favourite flowers, prune trees to suit their needs, and dig up and destroy plants they either do not like or like too much.

I once saw a female leprechaun tear out several hop plants by the roots because her mate had taken too much of a liking to brewing beer. He was either always drunk, or always brewing. She was tired of being ignored. She destroyed his stock of beer and tore out the hops he used to flavour it.

The leprechaun eventually got back into brewing but kept it as a hobby and made sure he paid enough attention to his mate. He also learned that if he gave her some beer, it was quite alright to get drunk together. Since her tolerance was lower than his, she would disappear early into the burrow to sleep it off and he could enjoy the rest of his beer alone. Nature achieves a balance.

Even mundane animals can contribute to ongoing garden maintenance. One year, a neighbour planted twenty beautiful parrot tulips that changed colour several times during their three-week blooming period. I was enchanted. The following spring, I was surprised to see two of these fabulous tulips growing in my own garden. The faeries informed me the culprit for the tulip theft was none other than a common squirrel! I must say, I was very pleased.

It is nice to introduce new species of plants now and again, and sometimes our older plants begin to take up more room in the garden than we would like. It is time to propagate!

Many common plants, like rhubarb, hemerocallis, monarda, mint, oregano, echinacea, sempervivum and sedums, can be propagated by taking a rooted 'baby' plant that is growing alongside the mother plant. This is by far the easiest propagation method with an almost guaranteed rate of success. By using this method you can also increase plant density in the garden. Or you can plant the baby into a pot and gift it to a friend.

If your friend is a gardener too, they will soon reciprocate with a rooted baby of their own. It is an unspoken link that forms between fellow gardeners. If you continue along this path for a few years, you will soon find yourself with a diverse garden—without having to spend more money!

To get the baby plant, sometimes it is growing far enough away from the mother (like in the case of raspberry canes) that you can dig up the baby and leave the mother undisturbed. If the division process is happening deeper underground, as is the case with Asiatic Lilies, you will have to dig up the entire plant. This tends to be called dividing, and rhubarb, hostas, and daylilies (hemerocallis) require this attention every six years or so. In this instance, the whole plant is removed from the soil.

This involves digging around the root mass until it is loose enough to lift the plant out of the soil. Then, the gardener carefully teases apart the roots until they have individual plants (sometimes what began as one plant can turn into ten pups or more). If you lack patience, you could brutishly slice the roots apart with a spade until you have divided it into two or three clumps.

Once divided, you take one of the new plants and re-plant it where the original mother plant was. Be sure to take this opportunity to incorporate some composted manure into the soil before you fill the hole back up. The other little plants can be potted and gifted, sold, or they can be planted elsewhere in your garden. Maybe you want to use them to further expand the habitat space in your yard!

The other method of propagation I most commonly recommend is propagation by cuttings. This is a great method to use with fruiting bushes and also works delightfully well with herbs. One begins by taking a cutting of a branch. Usually softer green wood is easier to propagate but different species of trees actually have their own preferences. If there is a specific tree you want to propagate, you can take a moment to verify which time of year and what age the wood should be before you get started.

In general, in the garden, cuttings should not be older than one year and propagation usually happens in the spring. When you have your cuttings, you can place the twig cut-end down into moist soil. Some plants root more readily than others, so I recommend dipping the cut-end into a rooting potion before inserting it into the soil. This will increase the likelihood of success.

Finally, the crudest, most mundane form of propagation is to propagate by seed. This is such a primitive form of planting that even an ogre with half a brain could figure it out.

If anyone tells you that I only look down my nose at this particular form of propagation because I am so bad at it that nearly every year my seedlings rot; I would ask you to send me that person's name. I would like to send them a very special package of maggots.

Planting by seed should be a no-brainer, but some seeds require a period of freezing temperatures or stratification to grow. Others need to remain perfectly moist for three weeks before they germinate. As if I had the patience!

WARNING

While it is tempting to share cuttings with Mundunce neighbours and friends, I would implore any responsible witch or mage not to go trading plants classified by Puriculus Primperton as "DANGEROUS TO MUNDUNCES". Such trading is against every law that I am aware of, in every magical locale that I am familiar with.

Chapter Six

Indoor Garden

I HOPE THIS BOOK WILL have provided you with the basic tools to improve an existing garden. My editor pointed out that I had given almost no notice to the gardener with little space in the first edition. I will address that gardener now; all you can do is introduce as many potted plants as you can in the space you have. Provide habitats, like wooden huts, bats boxes, rock piles. The same advice that you have received at every step throughout this book can be adapted and applied to the humblest balcony or window box.

For the indoor gardener, I am sorry to say it is entirely impractical for you to hope faeries or other creatures will want to live inside your home with you. For one, your pet cat or dog would likely try to eat them. But they are also repulsed by the smell of humans and our cooking. They will most definitely destroy all your belongings when you leave your house.

The indoor gardener is better served by maintaining indoor plants for their own pleasure. You will have the satisfaction of knowing that in some tiny, minuscule way those plants are sequestering carbon so that the creatures outdoors may enjoy a little more time before a climate catastrophe destroys us all. Greenery indoors is calming and meditative—it has been shown to improve the mood of witching folk who take the time to have a few house plants.

I recommend Pothos as the king of indoor plants; they come in several varieties with different colours, they grow well in most conditions, and they are forgiving if one is inconsistent with watering. Pothos are also known as money plants in some parts of the world. If your money plant is growing, so is your money!

The second must-have indoor plant is Aloe Vera. This is edible and an excellent natural source of vitamin B12. The gel is effective at soothing burns. Anyone who accidentally gets a good sunburn will feel instant relief when the gel is applied to the burned area. My spouse burns himself in the kitchen at least once a month. With the presence of Aloe Vera, the pain is quickly soothed.

Finally, spider plants bring luck and good health to the home (as well as being visually pleasing in a hanging pot). They are easy to propagate, come in several varieties, and are very difficult to kill.

If you have an old glass tank handy, you can have an indoor aquatic garden. There is an exciting trend to create mini aquascapes that are breath-taking. You can create the look of above-ground natural landscapes in the water, or create natural-looking river habitats with driftwood and algae.

What most excites me about this type of project is that even a seasoned gardener has access to a whole new world of aquatic plants! They are just as varied as those above ground. Some look like mosses, ferns, grasses, and they come in reds, greens, and blues.

Once you have placed the aquascape, planted the plants, and let the water rest for a month, you can add grindylows and tiny kelpies into the tank where they can hide among the plants and interact with the landscape. I like to put in a few shrimp and snails too, to keep the tank clean. Remember you will need a filtration system to keep the water flowing! Just make sure your cat does not go fishing for kelpies!

Bonus: you can use the dirty water to water your plants. It is full of nutrients that will make your houseplants grow lush and strong. Now that is something!

Creature Glossary

List of featured magical beings:

Ashray: Translucent creature that spends its time in the water. It reflects moonlight and thus is only ever seen by night. Rather like a large salamander, but glows light blue.

Bigfoot: Historically eight to ten feet tall. Due to habitat loss and in-breeding, modern purebred bigfoot reach an average height of six and a half feet. Shaggy, muddy-brown fur covers their bodies. Their skin is a sandy, tanned colour. Reasonable intelligence. Bigfoot are gifted singers and use their voices to create unique magic through vibrational resonance.

Brownie: Nocturnal creatures who tidy up scraps, clippings, and other garden waste. Though they are the same height as gnomes, brownies are lean and slender. Probably because their diet is garbage.

Bunyip: Wolf-like in size and appearance, this creature has two long protruding fangs. They live in swamps and waterways, their howls are heard for kilometers around. I have never met one I liked. They will devour any living thing that approaches their aquatic home, making them rather poor company in a garden designed to encourage creatures to inhabit.

Cat-Sith: These small black cats wander in areas where massacres or battles have occurred. More common in older countries where there have been thousands of years of human conflict. These black cats with a white spot on their chest spread around the globe with human conquerors. It is believed the spirit is created by the agony of mothers losing their children in conflict.

Celestial Fish: These red fish grow slightly larger than koi fish. Red spines protrude from the fin on the fish's back. They will float a little over the surface of the water to munch on fireflies and other insects before floating back down below the surface of the water.

Chimaera: A fire breathing beast with a lion's head, a goat protruding from its back, and some are said to have a snake instead of a tail. These beasts are huge—approximately the same size as an African elephant. They are reputed to have fierce tempers and are strongly associated with evil. I have lots of Catswort planted on my property, which attracts them, and these huge creatures are very docile once they have rolled around in the plants for a little while. Due to their huge size, I cannot encourage it to stay but it is a treat to see one cross my path every few years.

Chupacabra: The size of a German Sheppard, these creatures look like dogs mixed with rodents and are completely hairless. They are nocturnal and prey on animals as large as goats. Contrary to popular belief, they are very pleasant and social creatures. I do not mind them as long as they do not go after one of the unicorns in my yard. They can have all the groundhogs they want.

Dragon: There are water dragons and winged dragons. Typically, these overgrown reptiles are so large and dangerous I would not recommend approaching them or offering them a refuge. However, most of the letters I get about attracting magic creatures include several questions about attracting dragons. Hence, they are included in this guide. Beware.

Faery: Only an inch larger than pixies, faeries are much more handsome. Their large, elegant wings glitter with bright colours and their visage is akin to beautiful feminine humans. They are intelligent enough for conversation and use pollen to dye their dark hair golden yellow.

Faun: Upper body of a human, the lower half of a goat. With two horns on their heads, these are peaceful creatures that roam pastures and woodlands. Highly intelligent, worth inviting to a cup of tea. They speak in terms of nature and seasons, and their temperament is very pleasant.

Fire bird: The size of a goose, looks as though it is made of flame but lacks the crackling heat of real fire. Fond of apples.

Fire toad: A large toad that spits fire to cook its prey. These creatures live in underground burrows and are a wonderful addition to any garden.

Flaming Gecko: Similar to a common gecko, these creatures enjoy rolling around in live embers. You can watch them while roasting marshmallows as they dart around beneath the flames.

Gnome: Fat, hard-headed fellows. They stand at about eight inches in height and often disguise themselves as stones in order to hide. They steal a lot of vegetables, but they can also be seen protecting crops from crows.

Goblin: Ugly humanoid creatures with a bitter, resentful nature. Lazy until it comes time to swindle you out of property or coin.

Grindylow: These tiny creatures, not more than three inches in height, will attempt to drown anyone that enters the water. They typically live on a diet of insect larvae and tadpoles. They are useful for keeping the mosquito population down and are funny little fellows if kept in a fish tank where you can watch them go about their daily business.

Harpy: A woman's head and torso on the body of a bird. They are generally considered bad luck and evil creatures of destruction. After a long conversation with a harpy, I learned she was in fact the victim of very nasty spell-work done by a jealous warlock whose hand she had refused. In addition to being cursed to bare her breasts and become part-bird, she is cursed with immortality. Long live the harpies.

Kappa: Rather like a small turtle, these creatures do bite and live on the same diet as the aforementioned grindylow. Only considered a magic creature due to Mundunce's inability to see them.

Kelpie: The front of the body resembles a horse, but the back is a large scaly tail designed to make the kelpie an excellent swimmer. There are many subspecies; some are as large as a horse, others as small as a seahorse. Some might actually be seahorses, it is difficult to tell them apart.

Leprechaun: Intelligent creatures, I enjoy conversing with them when I do my weeding. Leprechauns live quiet lives of cultivation. The four square feet I have given over to the leprechaun couple who live in my garden are always well tended, weeded, and productive.

Luminescent Snake: These snakes have stripes that reflect moonlight. Thus, they glow. Not particularly magical. Due to their diet of nymphs and pixies they are far more common in a witch or warlock's garden than in the garden of a Mundunce.

Manticore: About the size of a horse, this feline creature has a scorpion-like tail which is very efficient for killing prey. Reputed to be evil but very docile when greeted with Catswort.

Minotaur: The head of a bull and the body of a very muscular human. You will likely find these in your garden if you have topiaries or a small labyrinth. They are shy herbivores and do not typically interact with humans. When you do see them, they are disarmingly attractive.

Nymph: (wood and/or water) A name for the immature form of many insect pests, and also a name for earthly deities. Here we discuss the common nymph; a feminine creature that melts into nature itself. They are bewildering and wonderful to see. Not dangerous, just mystifying.

Ogre: Large creatures, reputed to eat human children. I do my best not to provide these beasts with any space in my garden. Do not approach under any circumstances without first alerting your local magical authority.

Phoenix: This legendary bird is extremely rare. Since phoenixes are shy, they are hardly ever seen. They can resurrect from their own ashes when they burn up at death. They live hundreds of years.

Pixie: Barely three inches tall, slender wings which hum while in flight, their narrow wrinkled features give pixies a look of perpetual resting-witch-face. Mischievous, will destroy plants they do not like. They hide in tall grasses and drink nectar from flowers.

Sphinx: The size of a lion with a wingspan reaching four meters and the head of a human. These felines are gentle giants, quiet guardians, and very affectionate. I once befriended a sphinx and she began to bring me gifts of dead wild turkeys when she visited.

Sprite: (wood and/or water) Translucent in appearance, these spirits attach themselves to waterways or trees. They will leave the safety of their shelter to forage for food but will hardly ever be seen further that a few meters from their home. It may take time for sprites to establish themselves in a new area, but once there they will live as long as the tree or waterway they inhabit.

Troll: Hostile creatures which can be hired by witching folk to harass others and instigate conflict.

Unicorn: Modern unicorns are no larger than a goat. They are known for their long horn and are as elusive as they are beautiful. You will know your garden is truly a safe-haven when you are blessed with a visit from these gentle creatures.

Yeti: Historically five to seven feet tall with thick torsos. Yeti are covered in white fur and their skin is black as coal. Due to inbreeding, modern yeti rarely grow taller than four feet. Blindness has become common among the population. These creatures are gifted in the arts of making plants grow quickly and manipulating light. Yeti are shy and adapted to camouflage. They are rarely seen.

Conclusion

THANK YOU FOR TAKING this journey with me. I hope you have learned something new and will be on your way to creating a garden fit for many creatures. If you felt entertained while reading this guide, it would be a tremendous help if you could take the time to rate it and recommend it to a friend.

Those of you who have graduated from Kentree Institute of Magic, perhaps you could put in a good word from me with Principal Crinwere. It is time Kentree offered a course in MagiZoogeography.

Blessed be.

-Alfurius Iltorpinder Lethridge Ebruli Starlange, a.k.a., A. ILES

Don't miss out!

Visit the website below and you can sign up to receive emails whenever A. Iles publishes a new book. There's no charge and no obligation.

https://books2read.com/r/B-A-VPYDB-IHIYE

BOOKS 2 READ

Connecting independent readers to independent writers.

Also by A. Iles

Kentree Series
Kentree's Stolen Souls

Standalone
Garden for Magic Creatures

9 798822 759602 4